Crayola
WINTER COLORS

Jodie Shepherd

Lerner Publications ◆ Minneapolis

Official Licensed Product
Lerner Publications Company
A division of Lerner Publishing Group, Inc.
241 First Avenue North
Minneapolis, MN 55401 USA

For reading levels and more information, look up this title at www.lernerbooks.com.

Main body text set in Billy Infant Regular 24/36.
Typeface provided by SparkyType.

Library of Congress Cataloging-in-Publication Data

Names: Shepherd, Jodie.
Title: Crayola winter colors / by Jodie Shepherd.
Description: Minneapolis : Lerner Publications, [2018] | Series: Crayola seasons | Audience:
   Age 4-9. | Audience: K to grade 3. | Includes bibliographical references and index.
Identifiers: LCCN 2016046974 (print) | LCCN 2016048156 (ebook) | ISBN 9781512432930
   (lb : alk. paper) | ISBN 9781512455762 (pb) | ISBN 9781512449327 (eb pdf)
Subjects: LCSH: Winter—Juvenile literature. | Seasons—Juvenile literature. | Crayons—
   Juvenile literature.
Classification: LCC QB637.8 .S54 2018 (print) | LCC QB637.8 (ebook) | DDC 535.6—dc23

LC record available at https://lccn.loc.gov/2016046974

Manufactured in the United States of America
1-41824-23784-1/24/2017

TABLE OF CONTENTS

THE WONDERS OF WINTER

The sky is gray. The ground is white.
Hats and scarves can be any color.

Winter is here!

Snow covers the ground like a white blanket.

A winter sunset shows off a blue and purple sky.

Fluffy snow piles on pointy green pine needles.

You can draw snowy trees. Give them texture by drawing sharp lines with a green crayon to make pine needles. Make squiggly lines with a brown crayon to look like tree bark.

Icicles sparkle
like diamonds.

You can draw icicles with shading. Start by using a dark color for the edge of the icicles. Then round them out with a lighter color.

ANIMALS IN WINTER

The bright red beak and feathers on this cardinal make it *pop* against the snowy branches.

Bright colors stand out from dull colors.
Which of these colors do you think stand
out the most?

WINTER FUN

Snow is awesome for slipping, sliding, and sledding.

What's your favorite wintertime activity?

A snowman's life is short. He'll be gone when the snow melts!

Design your own snowman. Stack circles for the snowman's body. Add a triangle for the nose.

What other shapes can you use?

Winter colors are inside too!

Gingerbread houses can be decorated with red, green, yellow, and more. What colors would you use?

Nothing is more colorful
than winter holidays!
Spread holiday cheer with
lights and ribbons.

What colors
do you use to
celebrate winter?

WORLD OF COLORS

Winter has many colors. Here are some of the Crayola® crayon colors used in this book. Can you find them in the photos?

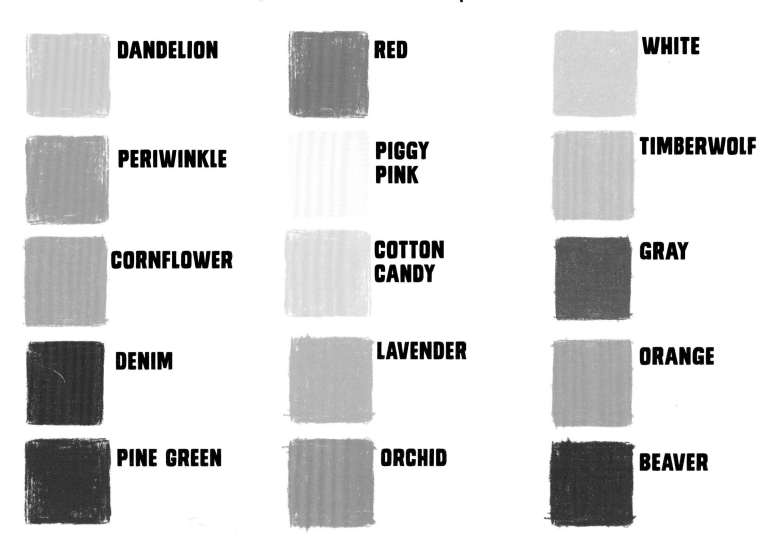

DANDELION

RED

WHITE

PERIWINKLE

PIGGY PINK

TIMBERWOLF

CORNFLOWER

COTTON CANDY

GRAY

DENIM

LAVENDER

ORANGE

PINE GREEN

ORCHID

BEAVER

GLOSSARY

bark: the outer layer that covers the trunk of a tree

design: to make a plan for creating something

dull: not bright or colorful

icicle: a hanging piece of ice formed by dripping water that freezes

pine needle: the thin, sharp leaf of a pine tree

shading: the use of dark areas in a drawing

squiggly: wavy and twisted, with many curves

texture: the look and feel of an object

TO LEARN MORE

BOOKS

Goldstone, Bruce. *Wonderful Winter*. New York: Henry Holt, 2016.
Explore fun facts about winter, and find ideas for winter crafts and winter holiday celebrations.

Moon, Walt K. *Winter Is Fun!* Minneapolis: Lerner Publications, 2017. Learn more about the changes in winter.

Snow, Virginia Brimhall. *Winter Walk*. Layton, UT: Gibbs Smith, 2014. Read this fun wintry story filled with craft ideas, trivia, and colorful drawings.

WEBSITES

Snowflake Stencils
http://www.crayola.com/crafts/snowflake-stencils-craft/
Design your own snowflakes. Cut them out, and hang them up to decorate your home this winter!

Winter Memory
http://kids.nationalgeographic.com/games/quick-play/winter-memory/
Play a wintry memory game at this website. Test your skills on the easy, medium, or hard levels!

INDEX

PHOTO ACKNOWLEDGMENTS

The images in this book are used with the permission of: © alexsol/Shutterstock.com, p. 1; © iStockphoto.com/Toltek, p. 2; © iStockphoto.com/shironosov, p. 5; © iStockphoto.com/sara_winter, pp. 6–7; © iStockphoto.com/AVTG, p. 8; © iStockphoto.com/Viorika, p. 10; © Tony Campbell/Shutterstock.com, p. 12; © Sergey Novikov/Shutterstock.com, p. 15; © FamVeld/Shutterstock.com, p. 16; © Ariel Skelley/Blend Images/Getty Images, pp. 18–19; © iStockphoto.com/Viktor_Gladkov, pp. 20–21.

Cover: © Brian Walter/Dreamstime.com (berries); © iStockphoto.com/AVTG (snow covered trees).

LERNER SOURCE

Expand learning beyond the printed book. Download free, complementary educational resources for this book from our website, www.lernerresource.com.